PRAYING WITH SAINT FRANCIS

Praying with
SAINT FRANCIS

Translated by

Regis J. Armstrong, OFM, CAP

and

Ignatius C. Brady, OFM

Introduction by

the Rev. Canon David Ford

William B. Eerdmans Publishing Company
Grand Rapids, Michigan

The prayers of St. Francis translation © 1982 by the
Missionary Society of St. Paul the Apostle in the State of New York

Selection and Introduction © 1987 by the
Society for Promoting Christian Knowledge
All rights reserved

First published 1987 in the U.K. by
Triangle
SPCK
Holy Trinity Church
Marylebone Road
London, NW1 4DU

This edition published 1996
in the United States of America
through special arrangement with SPCK by
Wm. B. Eerdmans Publishing Co.
255 Jefferson Ave. S.E., Grand Rapids, Michigan 49503

Printed in the United States of America

01 00 99 98 97 96   7 6 5 4 3 2 1

Library of Congress Cataloging-in-Publication Data

Francis, of Assisi, Saint, 1182-1226
[Selections. English. 1996]
Praying with Saint Francis / translated by Regis J. Armstrong
and Ignatius C. Brady : introduction by David Ford.
p.   cm.
Originally published: London : Triangle : SPCK, 1987.
ISBN 0-8028-4271-2 (pbk. : alk. paper)
1. Francis, of Assisi, Saint, 1182-1226 — Prayer-books
and devotions — English. I. Armstrong, Regis J.
II. Brady, Ignatius C. III. Title.
BX4700.F61E5   1996
242'.802 — dc21   96-48115
CIP

The publisher gratefully acknowledges permission to reprint from
copyrighted works granted by the publishers listed on p. 70.

CONTENTS

Introduction *by the Rev. Canon David Ford*   vii

The Life of St Francis of Assisi   xii

THE CANTICLE OF THE SUN   1

IN PRAISE OF GOD   5

OUR LORD AND FATHER   19

WORSHIP HIM WITH PSALMS   31

MEDITATE ON HIS WORD   61

Acknowledgements   70

INTRODUCTION

There are moments when, suddenly, in literature, history, and in Holy Scripture, a piercing glimmer of truth darts out at us, and something which we have known for a long time, and perhaps taken for granted, pricks our hearts and minds into a new realisation and a deeper awareness of that truth.

One of these darts is contained in the book of Ecclesiastes, chapter 7, verse 29: 'God made us plain and simple, but we have made ourselves very complicated' (GNB).

Another of these darts of truth is the man we call St Francis of Assisi. He directs us very firmly back to the Truth of God. His special spirituality has brought, and still brings, millions of men and women face to face with the theological truth that 'All things come from God, and of his own do we give him.'

The popular sentimental picture of a man talking to birds and animals has tended to make St Francis seem unreal, and unrelated to everyday life as we know it. Like the pictures of the Devil with horns and tail, and angels with haloes, the unreality of the image has tended to persuade twentieth-century people towards a fairytale idea of the Christian faith — enjoyable but nothing to do with the real world. The exact opposite is the case, of course, and Francis, perhaps more than any other saint, teaches us that to be a disciple of Jesus Christ is not to be concerned with fantasies or with passing fashions of thought, but with the eternal truth that God is: God created everything; God loves his creation.

His love of nature is not therefore a sentimental love of God's dumb animals, but rather an acute awareness of the interrelationship of all living creatures; and this 'oneness' is seen in our total dependency on our loving Creator. Thus, far from being a rather weak, ineffectual person (who to some might appear 'soft'), his firm and unflinching trust proclaims that every human action is relevant to God and to God's creation. This witness makes him one of the most powerful men who has ever lived; powerful, not in a materialistic sense but in the spiritual sense which has to do with the 'inner life' rather than with outward appearances.

Francis is first and foremost a man of prayer. He shows from his prayers and meditations how actions and attitudes radiate through life, and life radiates through prayer. He teaches that what is within our hearts clearly reflects in our lives, and that the depth of our inner perception controls our deeds and actions.

His own life radiated humility, love and joy. The poverty which he valued so much may be seen as the outcome of his reverence for the integrity of creation. As God does not manipulate the universe from outside to accomplish his will, but works from within, Francis was obedient to God and refused to possess, exploit or manage the world to suit his own wishes. By possessing no personal and no material goods he demonstrated a freedom from self-desire and achieved true humility.

The spirit of chastity created in him a dedication

of his whole being to God, and resulted in a powerful and loving attitude to all God's creation — a reflection of God's love.

Obedience was seen not as a passive acceptance of others' dictates, but as an active offering of all his abilities and energies, participating in the common life of the world. By following such a path, Francis showed his joyful abandonment to God.

These powerful weapons of God, far stronger than any weapons of this world, were expressed daily in Francis' life, and clearly fuelled by God through an inner life of prayer. Many, many hours of prayer were offered. They were never forgotten or overlooked, which was why he was able to regard the sun and moon, water, wind and bodily death as his brothers and sister; as his relations in one big family. He really believed that God has made us plain and simple, and he refused to be complicated.

This is the reason why Francis has so much attraction for both Catholic and Protestant Christians alike. His simplicity unites all Christians in the love of God, in every generation. His theological insight requires hours of meditation until the deepest truths sink into the depths of our souls. He is as aware of life's complications as anyone who has lived, and yet his obedient, loving trust, radiating joy and humility, shows us the way to follow Christ. His spirituality lifts all things to infinite value and, rather than bringing God down to our level, raises all creation up to its Creator. He enjoys a wonderful personal communication with the Lord which combines an ease and joy with reverence and honour; never over-friendly or overestimating his own importance, while accepting his own importance in the context of all creation — loved by God.

G. K. Chesterton wrote that 'No pope or beggar, sultan or robber, could look into the eyes of St Francis without feeling that the saint had a real interest in him and in his inner life.' Millions of Christians still feel this as they read his story.

The Church in the early thirteenth century was in great danger of secularisation. Francis' emphasis on absolute poverty — which brought together the brotherhood of monks later known as the Franciscan Order — has sometimes been described as the salvation of the Church. Again it was the 'plain and simple' which overpowered the 'complicated'.

In his comparatively short life, Francis knew severe physical suffering and also faced a great deal of personal misunderstanding and opposition. On 14 September 1224, while praying and fasting alone in a mountain retreat, he received the stigmata, the marks of the Lord's wounds, on his own body; an outward and physical sign of the inward and spiritual power of God working within this simple person. He died on 3 October 1226 at the age of forty-four, lying on the bare floor and refusing a covering, in complete poverty.

Less than two years later the Pope accepted him among the saints. The ceremony took place not in Rome but in Assisi, and the Pope spoke these words:

He was like the morning star in the clouds.
He was like the full moon when in evidence.
He was like the sun with all its rays.
That is the way he shone in the temple of God.

No one who has ever visited Assisi can fail to notice that 'something' in the atmosphere of the place, despite the grandeur of the basilica, the crowds, the tourist industry and the twentieth-century influences. Through it all permeates the quiet and gentle spirit of St Francis, who calls us all to God. That is why we would all do well to pray these prayers — again and again — until we too meet Sister Death of the body. And that is why we would do well to listen to the secret of St Francis and of Holy Scripture: 'God made us plain and simple, but we have made ourselves very complicated.'

*　　*　　*

This book contains nearly all the known prayers of St Francis as well as the Psalms from the Office of the Passion and also meditations taken from his writings and admonitions. The prayers can be a help to those who lead public worship, but they can especially be used in private devotion. For instance, in the Office of the Passion, there are fourteen offerings of praise: all verses chosen from the book of Psalms but marvellously put together in such a way as to place us looking to God our Heavenly Father and in simplicity offering him our praise. Some people might like to mark off each Psalm and say one every morning and another every evening, making a weekly cycle of praise.

David Ford
Ripon Cathedral
April 1987

THE LIFE OF
ST FRANCIS OF ASSISI

Francis of Assisi was born in 1182 and died in 1226.
Of his comparatively short life, less than twenty
years were spent in active Christian ministry; yet by
the time of his death, brothers of the Order which
he founded had travelled through much of Europe,
the Mediterranean area and North Africa, and the
order had already had its first martyrs.

The story of Francis' conversion is well known
— how as a young man in his early twenties he
abandoned a life of ease and comfort to embrace the
Lady Poverty. Giotto's paintings on the walls of the
basilica in Assisi where the saint lies buried, graphi-
cally illustrate incidents from his early life.

Typical of the fashionable youth of his time,
Francis was imbued with the romantic spirit of
chivalry. He took part enthusiastically in the fight-
ing between the warring city states of central Italy,
and was eventually captured and held prisoner for
a year in the neighbouring city of Perugia. During
this time he became severely ill. Ransomed by his
father, a wealthy cloth merchant, he returned home
to Assisi, but he never regained his former health
and high spirits. In 1204, on the eve of setting out
once more to battle, he experienced a vision which
caused him to abandon his ambitions for military
glory and to espouse a life of poverty.

It was while Francis was praying before the crucifix in the near derelict church of San Damiano, outside the walls of Assisi, that he heard a voice telling him to 'rebuild my church'. With typical enthusiasm he took this literally, sold some bales of cloth from his father's warehouse and donated the proceeds to the parish priest. This impulsive action led to his being publicly disowned by his father, whereupon, in a dramatic gesture, he stripped himself naked before the assembled populace of Assisi, symbolising his break with the past. 'Henceforth,' he declared, 'I shall say "My Father who art in heaven", not "My father Pietro Bernadone".'

From then on, Francis lived as a mendicant, owning nothing but a rough tunic, begging or working at menial tasks for his food. His particular concern was for the outcasts of society. When he encountered a beggar who was suffering from leprosy, the disease which above all inspired horror in the respectable people of those days, he forced himself to overcome his natural repugnance, embraced the man and gave him his tunic. Subsequently he went to live for some months with a colony of leprosy sufferers near Gubbio.

In 1208, while attending Mass on St Matthias' day, Francis heard read the Gospel for the day:

And as you go, preach the message, 'The kingdom of heaven is at hand.' Cure the sick, raise the dead, cleanse the lepers, cast out devils. Freely you have received, freely give. Do not keep gold, silver or money in your girdles, no wallet for your journey, nor two tunics, no sandals, nor staff; for the labourer deserves his living (Matthew 10.7-10).

Instantly, Francis recognised God's call in these words of Scripture. It was the way of life for which he had been searching. It was the way he was to follow, quite literally in every particular, till the day of his death.

He embarked at once on a preaching ministry, and was soon joined by the first few of his companions. Together they travelled to Rome, to obtain the Pope's approval for a simple Rule for the embryo Order. The small church of the Portiuncola at St Mary of the Angels near Assisi which the brothers rebuilt with their own hands, became their base, from which they constantly travelled on preaching missions to the surrounding countryside.

The Order of Friars Minor grew rapidly, and was soon sending missions beyond Italy to other countries in the Mediterranean area. Francis himself travelled to Spain, Dalmatia and, most dramatically, to the Holy Land and to Damietta in Egypt, where there took place his famed encounter with the Sultan in 1219, during the time of the Fifth Crusade. The first mission to England took place in 1224.

During these years Francis was suffering from increasing ill-health, particularly from deteriorating eyesight and from ulcers on his legs and feet (it has been suggested that he may have been diabetic). In 1220 he gave up to another the leadership of the Order, though he continued to make preaching tours throughout central Italy, seated on a donkey or carried in a litter. His influence within the Order remained strong, and when the Rule was revised and rewritten in 1221 (in this book referred to as the

'Earlier Rule'), and again in 1223, it contained passages of exhortation and admonition which clearly originated with Francis himself.

It was in September 1224 that Francis received the stigmata, while keeping a forty-day fast at a mountain hermitage at La Verna. Thereafter he became progressively more ill, almost blind and unable to walk without pain. It was recorded of him that 'he could not bear the light of the sun during the day or the light of the fire at night. He constantly remained in darkness inside the house in his cell. His eyes caused him so much pain that he could neither lie down nor sleep' (*The Legend of Perugia*). Yet, according to tradition, it was at this time that he wrote the *Canticle of the Sun*, with its praise of Brother Sun and Brother Fire.

It is Francis' love of nature, epitomised in the *Canticle*, which has most endeared him to modern Christians, to the neglect of other aspects of his spirituality. Yet his love of all created things was simply an extension of his deep love of the Creator. His biographer, Thomas of Celano, wrote of him not many years after his death:

In every work of the artist he praised the Artist; whatever he found in the things made he referred to the Maker. He rejoiced in all the works of the hands of the Lord and saw behind things pleasant to behold their life-giving reason and cause. In beautiful things he saw Beauty itself; all things were to him good. 'He who made us is the best,' they cried out to him. Through his footprints impressed upon things he followed the Beloved everywhere;

he made for himself from all things a ladder by which to come even to his throne.

He embraced all things with a rapture of unheard of devotion, speaking to them of the Lord and admonishing them to praise him. He spared lights, lamps and candles, not wishing to extinguish their brightness with his hand, for he regarded them as a symbol of Eternal Light. He walked reverently upon stones, because of him who was called the Rock . . .

He forbade the brothers to cut down the whole tree when they cut wood, so that it might have hope of sprouting again. He commanded the gardener to leave the border around the garden undug, so that in their proper times the greenness of the grass and the beauty of flowers might announce the Father of all things . . . he ordered that honey and the best wines be set out for the bees, lest they perish from want in the cold of winter.

Thomas of Celano, Second *Life,* cxxiv, 165

His failing health did not prevent Francis from continuing to visit towns and villages of Tuscany and Umbria, until the late summer of 1226 when, his condition grown worse, he was taken to the palace of the Bishop of Assisi. In late September, when it became clear that his death was imminent, he insisted on being carried down the hill to the Portiuncola. In the *Little Flowers of Saint Francis* there is an account of this last journey:

The friars took him up in their arms and carried him on the way toward St Mary of the Angels, accompanied by a crowd of people. When they reached a hospital that was on the way, St Francis asked whether they had arrived that far, because as a result of his extreme penance and former weeping, his eyesight was impaired and he could not see well. So when he was told that they were at the hospital, he said to those who were carrying him: 'Set me down on the ground and turn me toward Assisi.'

And standing in the road, with his face turned toward the city, he blessed it with many blessings, saying:

'May the Lord bless you, holy city, for through you many souls shall be saved, and in you many servants of God shall dwell, and from you many shall be chosen for the Kingdom of Eternal Life.'

And after he had said those words, he had himself carried farther on to St Mary of the Angels.

Francis died on 3rd October, 1226. As he lay awaiting death, he asked the brothers to sing psalms of praise, in which he himself joined as far as he was able. He requested that there be read to him the story of Christ's passion from St John's Gospel. Then, at list, in the words of Thomas of Celano, 'when many brothers had gathered about . . . his most holy soul was freed from his body and received into the abyss of light, and his body fell asleep in the Lord.'

*　　*　　*

Among the writings of St Francis which have come down to us and which are quoted in this book are:

1205/6   The Prayer before the Crucifix

1213-21   The Letter to the Faithful (first version)

1219-21   The Letter to the Faithful (second version)

1221   The 'Earlier Rule'

1224   The Parchment given to Brother Leo

1225   The Letter to the Entire Order

1226   The Testament

Undated: The Admonitions

    The Exhortation to the Praise of God

    The Office of the Passion

    The Praises to be Said at All the Hours

    The Prayer Inspired by the Our Father

    The Salutation of the Virtues

It will be noted that the prayer 'Make me an instrument of your peace', which is commonly attributed to St Francis, is not included in this book. It is in fact of modern composition, and on comparison with the authentic prayers, the stylistic difference is immediately apparent.

THE CANTICLE
OF THE SUN

The Canticle of the Sun

Most High, all-powerful, good Lord,
Yours are the praises, the glory,
    the honour and all blessing.
To you alone, Most High, do they belong,
and no man is worthy to mention your name.

Praised be you, my Lord, with all
    your creatures,
especially Sir Brother Sun,
Who is the day, and through whom you
    give us light.
And he is beautiful and radiant with
    great splendour,
and bears a likeness of you, Most High One.

Praised be you, my Lord, through Sister Moon
    and the stars,
in heaven you formed them clear
    and precious and beautiful.

Praised be you, my Lord, through Brother Wind,
And through the air, cloudy and serene,
    and every kind of weather
through which you give sustenance to
    your creatures.

Praised be you, my Lord, through Sister Water,
which is very useful and humble and
    precious and chaste.

Praised be you, my Lord, through Brother Fire,
through whom you light the night,
and he is beautiful and playful and robust
  and strong.

Praised be you, my Lord, through our Sister
  Mother Earth,
who sustains and governs us,
and who produces varied fruits with
  coloured flowers and herbs.

Praised be you, my Lord, through those
  who give pardon for your love
and bear infirmity and tribulation.
Blessed are those who endure in peace
For by you, Most High, they shall be crowned.

Praised be you, my Lord, through our Sister
  Bodily Death,
from whom no living man can escape.
Woe to those who die in mortal sin.
Blessed are those whom death will find
  in your most holy will,
for the second death shall do them no harm.

Praise and bless my Lord, and give him thanks,
and serve him with great humility.

The *Canticle of the Sun* was composed within two years of Francis'
death, when he was already very ill. The stanza in praise of pardon
is said to have been added later, when Francis helped to reconcile
a feud between the Bishop of Assisi and the mayor of the town.
The stanza on Sister Bodily Death was composed shortly before
his own death at St Mary of the Angels on 4 October 1226.

IN PRAISE OF GOD

All-powerful, most holy, most high
and supreme God,
Holy and just Father,
Lord, King of heaven and earth,
we thank you for yourself
for through your holy will
and through your only Son
with the Holy Spirit
you have created all things
spiritual and corporal
and, having made us
in your own image and likeness,
you placed us in paradise.
And through our own fault we have fallen.

And we thank you
for as through your son you created us
so also, through your holy love,
with which you loved us,
you brought about his birth
as true God and true man
by the glorious, ever-virgin,
most blessed, holy Mary,
and you willed to redeem us captives
through his cross and blood and death.

And we thank you
for your Son himself will come again
in the glory of his majesty
to send the wicked ones
who have not done penance
and who have not known you
into the eternal fire

and to say to all those who have known you
and have adored you,
and have served you in penance:
'Come, you blessed of my Father,
receive the kingdom,
which has been prepared for you
from the beginning of the world.'

And because all of us
wretches and sinners
are not worthy to pronounce your name,
we humbly ask that
our Lord Jesus Christ
in whom you were well pleased,
together with the Holy Spirit, the Paraclete,
give you thanks
as it pleases you and him
for everything.
He, who always satisfies you in everything,
through whom you have done
such great things for us. Alleluia!

From the 1221 *Rule of the Friars Minor,* 'One of the richest
spiritual documents of the Franciscan tradition'.

Holy, holy, holy
Lord God Almighty,
who is and
who was and
who is to come:

Let us praise and glorify him forever.

O Lord our God,
you are worthy
to receive praise
 and glory
 and honour
 and blessing:

Let us praise and glorify him forever.

The Lamb who was slain
is worthy
to receive power
 and divinity
 and wisdom
 and strength
 and honour
 and glory
 and blessing:

Let us praise and glorify him forever.

Let us bless the Father
and the Son
with the Holy Spirit:

Let us praise and glorify him forever.

Bless the Lord,
all you works of the Lord:

Let us praise and glorify him forever.

Sing praise to our God,
all you his servants
and you who fear God,
the small and the great:

Let us praise and glorify him forever.

Let heaven and earth praise
    him who is glorious:

Let us praise and glorify him forever.

And every creature
    that is in heaven
    and on earth
    and under the earth
    and in the sea
    and those which are in them:

Let us praise and glorify him forever.

Glory to the Father
and to the Son
and to the Holy Spirit:

Let us praise and glorify him forever.

As it was in the beginning
is now
and shall be forever. Amen.

Let us praise and glorify him forever.

All powerful, most holy,
most high and supreme God:
all good,
supreme good,
totally good,
you who alone are good;
may we give you
    all praise, all glory,
    all thanks, all honour,
    all blessings,
and all good things.

So be it.
So be it. Amen.

Revelation 4.8, 11; 5.12; Song of the Three Young Men 35;
Revelation 19.5; Psalm 69.34; Revelation 5.13.

The *Praises to be Said at All the Hours,* that is, at each of the
canonical Offices, in association with 'A Prayer Inspired by the
"Our Father"' (see p. 21).

11

Exhortation to the Praise of God

Fear the Lord and give him honour.
The Lord is worthy to receive praise and honour.
All you who fear the Lord, praise Him.

Heaven and earth, praise him.
All you rivers, praise him.

All you children of God, bless the Lord.

This is the day which the Lord has made,
Let us exalt and rejoice in it!
Alleluia, alleluia, alleluia! O King of Israel!

Let every spirit praise the Lord.
Praise the Lord for he is good;
All you who read this, bless the Lord;

All you creatures, bless the Lord.
All you birds of the heavens, praise the Lord.

All you children, praise the Lord.
Young men and virgins, praise the Lord.

The Lamb who was slain is worthy to receive
        praise,
glory, and honour.

Blessed be the holy Trinity and undivided Unity.

Revelation 14.7, 4.11, Psalms 22.23; 69.34; Song of the Three
Young Men 3.56, 60; Psalms 118.24; 150.6; 147.1; 103.20-21;

148.10; 113.1; 148.12; Revelation 5.12.

Said to have been written by Francis, together with drawings of various creatures, on a wooden panel now part of the altar in the hermitage of Cesi di Terni, Umbria.

You are holy, Lord, the only God,
You do wonders.

You are strong, you are great,
You are the most high.
You are the almighty King.
Holy, Holy Father, the King of heaven and earth.

You are Three and One, Lord God of gods;
You are good, all good, the highest good,
Lord, God, living and true.

You are love, charity.
You are wisdom;
You are humility;
You are patience;
You are beauty;
You are meekness;
You are security;
You are inner peace;
You are joy;
You are our hope and joy;
You are justice;
You are moderation;
You are all our riches;
You are enough for us;

You are beauty, you are meekness;
You are the protector,
You are our guardian and defender;
You are strength, you are refreshment.

You are our hope, you are our faith,
You are our charity,
You are all our sweetness,
You are our eternal life:
Great and wonderful Lord,
God almighty, Merciful Saviour.

From a parchment written by Francis in his own hand. In
September 1224, two years before his death, Francis kept a
forty-day fast at Mount La Verna, 'and the hand of the Lord
was laid upon him'. It was then that he received the stigmata,
and afterwards composed these praises, which he gave to
Brother Leo, together with his blessing (see p. 30).

Let us refer all good
　　to the most high and supreme Lord God,
and acknowledge that every good is his,
and thank him for everything,
　　he from whom all good things come.
And may he,
　　the Highest and Supreme,
　　who alone is true God,
have and be given and receive
　　every honour and reverence,
　　every praise and blessing,
　　every thanks and glory,
for every good is his,
　　he who alone is good.

From the 1221 *Rule of the Friars Minor*.

Let every creature
    in heaven, on earth,
    in the sea and in the depths,
give praise,
    glory, honour and blessing
to him
    who suffered so much for us,
    who has given so many good things,
    and who will continue to do so for the future.
For he is our power and strength,
    he who alone is good,
    who is most high,
    who is all-powerful, admirable and glorious;
    who alone is holy, praiseworthy, and blessed
    throughout endless ages.
    Amen.

From the *Letter to Faithful Christians* (second version): 'To all
Christian religious, clergy and laity, men and women, and to all
who live in the whole world'.

Let us bless the Lord,
the living and true God;
to him let us always render
     praise,
     glory,
     honour,
     blessing,
and every good.
Amen. Amen.
So be it. So be it.

From the *Office of the Passion*.

OUR LORD AND FATHER

Prayers and Exhortations

A Prayer Inspired by the 'Our Father'

OUR most holy FATHER,
Our Creator, Redeemer, Consoler, and Saviour,

WHO ART IN HEAVEN:
In the angels and in the saints,
Enlightening them to love, because you, Lord,
   are light,
Inflaming them to love, because you, Lord,
   are love,
Dwelling in them and filling them
   with happiness,
     because you, Lord, are the Supreme Good,
     the Eternal Good,
     from whom comes all good,
without whom there is no good.

HALLOWED BE YOUR NAME:
May our knowledge of you become ever
   clearer
That we may know
   the breadth of your blessings,
   the length of your promises,
   the height of your majesty,
   the depth of your judgements.

YOUR KINGDOM COME:
So that you may rule in us through
   your grace
and enable us to come to your kingdom
where there is an unclouded vision of you,
   a perfect love of you,

a blessed companionship with you,
an eternal enjoyment of you.

YOUR WILL BE DONE ON EARTH AS IT IS
IN HEAVEN:
That we may love you with our whole heart
    by always thinking of you,
    with our whole soul by always desiring you,
    with our whole mind by directing all our
            intentions to you
    and by seeking your glory in everything,
and with our whole strength by spending all our
    energies and affections
    of soul and body
    in the service of your love
    and of nothing else;
and may we love our neighbours as ourselves
    by drawing them all with our whole strength
            to your love,
    by rejoicing in the good fortunes of others as
            well as our own,
and by sympathising with the misfortunes
    of others,
and by giving offence to no one.

GIVE US THIS DAY:
In memory and understanding and reverence
    of the love which our Lord Jesus Christ
    had for us,
    and of those things which he said
    and did and suffered for us,

OUR DAILY BREAD:
Your own Beloved Son, our Lord Jesus Christ.

AND FORGIVE US OUR TRESPASSES:
Through your ineffable mercy
through the power of the Passion of your
        Beloved Son . . .

AS WE FORGIVE THOSE WHO TRESPASS
AGAINST US:
And whatever we do not forgive perfectly,
do you, Lord, enable us to forgive to the full,
so that we may truly love our enemies,
and fervently intercede for them before you,
returning no one evil for evil,
and striving to help everyone in you.

AND LEAD US NOT INTO TEMPTATION:
Hidden or obvious,
sudden or persistent.

BUT DELIVER US FROM EVIL:
Past, present and to come.

Glory to the Father and to the Son
    and to the Holy Spirit,
As it was in the beginning, is now,
    and shall be forever. Amen.

Francis had a great love for the Lord's Prayer and encouraged
its frequent use by the brothers, especially those who 'walking
in simplicity of spirit . . . did not know as yet the ecclesiastical
office'.

Most high,
   glorious God,
enlighten the darkness
   of my heart
and give me, Lord,
   a correct faith,
   a certain hope,
   a perfect charity,
   sense and knowledge,
so that I may carry out
your holy and true command.

The *Prayer before the Crucifix,* said to date from the time when
Francis, praying in the ruined church of San Damiano, heard
the voice of the Lord telling him to 'Go and repair my house.'

Almighty, eternal, just and merciful God,
   grant us in our misery and grace
to do for you alone
   what we know you want us to do,
and always
   to desire what pleases you.
Thus,
   inwardly cleansed,
   interiorly enlightened,
   and inflamed by the fire of the Holy Spirit,
may we be able to follow
   in the footprints of your beloved Son,
   our Lord Jesus Christ.
And,
by your grace alone,
may we make our way to you,
   Most High,
   Who live and rule
   in perfect Trinity and simple Unity,
   and are glorified,
   God all-powerful,
   forever and ever.
Amen.

From the *Letter to the Entire Order,* written probably near the end of his life.

Let us all love the Lord God
with all our heart, all our soul,
with all our mind and all our strength,
and with fortitude
and with total understanding,
with all of our powers,
with every effort,
every emotion,
every desire
and every wish.

He has given
    and gives to each of us
our whole body,
our whole soul
and our whole life.
He created us
and redeemed us,
and will save us
by his mercy alone.
He did and does
    every good thing for us,
who are miserable and wretched,
rotten and foul-smelling,
ungrateful and evil.

Therefore
let us desire nothing else.
let us wish for nothing else
let nothing else please us
    and cause us delight
except our Creator and Redeemer and Saviour,
the one true God,

Who is the Fullness of Good
   all good, every good,
   the true and supreme good,
Who alone is Good
   merciful and gentle,
   delectable and sweet,
Who alone is holy
   just and true
   holy and right,
Who alone is kind
   innocent
   pure,
from whom and through whom and in whom is
   all pardon
   all grace
   all glory
of all the penitent and the just
of all the blessed who rejoice together
   in heaven.

Therefore
let nothing hinder us
   nothing separate us
   or nothing come between us.
Let all of us
   wherever we are
   in every place
   at every hour
   at every time of day
   every day and continually
believe truly and humbly
and keep in our heart
and love, honour, adore, serve

praise and bless
glorify and exalt
magnify and give thanks to the most high and
     supreme eternal God
Trinity and Unity
the Father and the Son and the Holy Spirit
Creator of all
Saviour of all who believe in him
    and hope in him
    and love him
Who is
    without beginning and without end
    unchangeable, invisible,
    indescribable, ineffable,
    incomprehensible, unfathomable,
    blessed, worthy of praise,
    glorious, exalted on high, sublime,
    most high, gentle, lovable,
    delectable and totally desirable above all else
    forever. Amen.

From the 1221 *Rule of the Friars Minor*.

Let us love God
and adore him
with a pure heart
and a pure mind,
because he who seeks
   this above all else
has said:

The true worshippers will adore the Father
   in spirit and in truth.
For all those who worship him
   are to worship him
   in the spirit of truth.

And let us praise him
and pray to him
day and night,
   saying:

Our Father who art in heaven.

Since we should pray always
and never lose heart.

John 4.23-4; Matthew 6.9; Luke 18.1

From the *Letter to the Faithful*, second version.

Prayer on Entering Any Church

We adore you, Lord Jesus Christ, in all
your churches throughout the world,
and we bless you, for through your holy
cross you have redeemed the world.

From his *Testament*, 4.

Prayer on Greeting Another

May the Lord give you peace.

'In all his preaching, before he proposed the word of God to
those gathered about, he first prayed for peace for them, saying:
"The Lord give you peace." ' Thomas of Celano, First *Life*, 23.

Blessing for a Brother

May the Lord bless you and keep you;
May he show his face to you and be
    merciful to you.
May he turn his countenance to you and
    give you peace.
May the Lord bless you, Brother.

Numbers 6.27.

A personal blessing given to Brother Leo and written on a
parchment in Francis' own hand (see pp. 16-17)

WORSHIP HIM WITH PSALMS

The Office of the Passion

Cry out to the Lord with joy, all the earth!
    speak praise to his name;
give glory to his praise.

Say to God: How terrifying are
    your deeds, Lord;
in the vastness of your strength
    your enemies shall fawn upon you.

Let all the earth adore you
    and sing praise to you;
let us sing praise to your name.

Come, listen, and I will tell
    all of you who fear God
how much he has done for my soul.

To him I cried with my mouth,
and sounds of music were on my tongue.

And from his holy temple
    he heard my voice,
and my cry reached his ears.

Bless our Lord, you peoples,
and make the voice of his praise
    be heard.

And all the tribes of the earth
    shall be blessed in him,
all the nations shall proclaim him.

Blessed be the Lord, the God of Israel,
who alone does marvellous
  and great deeds.
And blessed forever be the name
  of his majesty,
and may all the earth be filled
  with his majesty.
Amen! Amen!

Psalms 66.1-4; 16-17; 18.6; 66.8; 72.17-19.

A psalm for Terce (mid-morning).

May the Lord hear you
   on the day of distress;.
may the name of the God of Jacob
   protect you.

May he send you help
   from his sanctuary,
and from Zion may he sustain you.

May he remember all of your sacrifices,
and may your burnt offering be fruitful.

May he grant you what your heart desires,
and may he fulfil your every plan.

May we rejoice in your victory,
and may we be victorious
   in the name of the Lord our God.

May the Lord fulfil all of your requests!
Now I know that the Lord sent
   his Son Jesus Christ,
and he will judge the peoples with justice.

And the Lord has become the refuge
   of the poor,
   a stronghold in times of distress;
and let them trust in you
   who know your name.

Blessed be the Lord my God,
   since he has become my stronghold
   and my refuge
in the day of my distress.

My helper, I will praise you,
for you, God, are my stronghold,
and my God, my mercy!

Psalms 20.1-5; 9.8-10; 144.1; 59.16-17.

A psalm for Sext (noon).

In you, Lord, I have hoped,
    let me never be put to shame;
in your fidelity, deliver me
    and rescue me.

Incline your ear to me,
save me.
be my protector, O God,
    and a stronghold,
that you may save me.

For you are my patience, Lord,
you are my hope, Lord, from my youth.

In you I have been supported from birth;
    from my mother's womb you are my protector,
and of you my song will always be.

May my mouth be filled with praise,
    that I may sing of your glory,
and all the day long of your greatness.

Answer me, Lord, for your mercy is kind;
look upon me out of the vastness
    of your mercies.

And hide not your face from your servant;
because I am in distress, make haste quickly,
make haste quickly to answer me.

Blessed be the Lord my God, for he has become
    my protector and my refuge
on the day of my distress.

O my helper, your praises will I sing,
for God is my protector,
   my God, my mercy.

Psalms 71.1-8; 69.16-17; 144.1; 59.16-17.

A psalm for None (mid-afternoon).

Psalms for Advent

How long, Lord, will you eternally forget me?
How long will you turn your face from me?

How long must I place doubts in my soul,
sorrow in my heart each day?

How long will my enemy rejoice over me?
Look, and hear me, O Lord my God.

Give light to my eyes
    that I may never sleep in death,
that my enemy may never say,
    I have overcome him.

Those who trouble me
    would rejoice if I stumbled,
but I have trusted in your kindness.

My heart shall rejoice in your saving help;
    I will sing to the Lord
    who has given good things to me,
and I will praise the name
    of the Lord most high.

Psalm 13.

A psalm for Compline (late evening).

I will praise you, Lord, most holy Father,
    King of heaven and earth,
for you have consoled me.

You are God my Saviour;
I will act confidently and not be afraid.

The Lord is my strength and my glory;
he has become my salvation.

Your right hand, O God, is magnificent
        in strength;
your right hand, O Lord, has shattered
        the enemy,
and in the vastness of your glory
    you have overthrown my enemies.

Let the poor see this and be glad;
seek God and your soul shall live.

Let heaven and earth praise him,
the sea and every living thing in them.

For God will save Zion,
and the cities of Judah will be rebuilt.

And they shall dwell there,
and they shall acquire it as their inheritance.

And the descendants of his servants
    shall possess it
and those who love his name
    shall dwell in it.

Isaiah 12.1-2; Exodus 15.6-7; Psalm 69.32-6.

A psalm for Matins (the first Hour of the day).

A Psalm for the Nativity

Ring out your joy to God our help,
and shout with cries of gladness
   to the Lord God living and true.

For the Lord, the most high, the awesome,
is the great king over all the earth.

For the most holy Father of heaven,
   our King before all ages,
has sent his beloved Son from on high
and he was born of the Blessed Virgin Mary.

He called upon me: you are my Father,
and I will enthrone him as the firstborn,
   the highest, above the kings of the earth.

On that day the Lord sent his mercy,
and at night his song was heard.

This is the day the Lord has made;
let us rejoice and be glad in it.

For the most holy beloved child was given to us,
   and he was born for us along the way
   and placed in a manger
since there was no room in the inn.

Glory to the Lord God in the highest,
and on earth peace to men of good will.

Let the heavens be glad and the earth rejoice,
  let the sea and all that is in it be moved,
let the fields and everything that is in them
  be joyful.

Sing a new song to him,
sing to the Lord, all the earth.

For the Lord is great and worthy of all praise
He is awesome, beyond all gods!

Give to the Lord, you families of nations,
  give to the Lord glory and praise;
give to the Lord the glory due to his name.

Offer your bodies and take up his holy cross
and follow his most holy commands even to
  the end.

Psalms 47.1-2; 74.12; 89.26-7; 42.8; 118.24; Isaiah 9.6; Luke 2.7,
14; Psalm 96.11-12, 1, 4, 7-8; Luke 14.27; 1 Peter 2.21.

Psalms of the Passion

God, I have told you of my life;
you have placed my tears in your sight.

All my enemies were planning evil things against
me;
and they have taken counsel together.

They repaid me evil for you,
and hatred for my love.

In return for my love they slandered me,
but I kept praying.

My holy Father, King of heaven and earth,
do not leave me,
since trouble is near and there is no one to help.

Let my enemies be turned back
on whatever day I shall call upon you;
for now I know that you are my God.

My friends and my neighbours have drawn near
and have stood against me;
and those who were close to me
have stayed far away.

You have driven my acquaintances far from me;
they have made me an abomination to them,
I have been handed over and I have not fled!

Holy Father, do not remove your help from me;
my God, look to my assistance.

Come to my help,
Lord, God of my salvation.

Glory to the Father and to the Son
    and to the Holy Spirit.
As it was in the beginning,
    is now, and shall be forever. Amen.

Psalms 56.8-9; 41.7; 71.10; 109.5; 109.4; John 17.11; Psalms 22.11; 56.9; 38.11; 88.8; John 17.11; Psalms 71.12; 38.22.

To be said at Compline on Holy Thursday. The psalm verses reflect our Lord's agony in the Garden of Gethsemane.

Lord, God of my salvation,
I cry to you by day and by night.

Let my prayer enter into your sight;
incline your ear to my prayer.

Look to my soul and free it;
ransom me from my enemies.

Since it is you who drew me out of the womb,
    you, my hope from my mother's breasts,
I am cast upon you from the womb.

From the womb of my mother you are my God;
do not depart from me.

You know my disgrace, and my confusion,
and my shame.

All those who trouble me are in your sight;
and my heart has expected abuse and misery.

And I looked for someone
    who would grieve together with me
    and there was none,
and for someone who would console me
    and I found none.

O God, the wicked have risen against me,
and they have sought my life
    in the assembly of the mighty,
and they have not placed you in their sight.

I am numbered among those who go down
 into the pit;
I have become as a man without help,
 free among the dead.

You are my most holy Father,
my King and my God.
Come to my help,
Lord, God of my salvation.

Psalms 88.1-2; 69.18; 22.9-11; 68.19-21; 86.14; 88.4-5; 44.4; 38.22.

A psalm for Matins. Christ's giving of himself in obedience to his Father.

Have mercy on me, O God, have mercy on me,
since my soul places its trust in you.

And I will hope as I stay
    under the shadow of your wings
until wickedness passes by.

I will cry to my most holy Father,
    the most high,
to the Lord, who has done good to me.

He has sent from heaven and delivered me;
he has disgraced those
    who have trampled upon me.

God has sent his mercy and his truth,
he has snatched my life
    from the strongest of my enemies
    and from those who hated me,
since they were too strong for me.

They have prepared a trap for my feet,
and have bowed down my soul.

They have dug a pit before my face,
and themselves have fallen into it.

My heart is ready, O God,
    my heart is ready;
I will sing and recite a psalm.

Arise, my glory, arise psalter and harp;
I will arise at dawn.

I will praise you among the peoples,
    O Lord,
I will say a psalm to you among the nations.

Since your mercy is exalted even to the skies,
and your truth even to the clouds.

Be exalted above the heavens, O God,
and may your glory be above all the earth!

Based on Psalm 57, with Psalm 18.17.

A psalm for Prime (early morning). Christ, appearing before
Pilate, places his confidence in God.

Have mercy on me, O God,
    for man has trampled me underfoot;
all the day long they have afflicted me
    and they fight against me.

My enemies trample upon me
    all the day long;
since those who wage war against me
    are many.

All my enemies have been thinking
    evil things against me;
they set an evil plan against me.

Those who guarded my life
have conspired together.

They went forth
and spoke together.

All those who see me laugh at me,
and they have spoken with their lips
    and have shaken their heads.

I am a worm, and no man;
the scorn of men
    and the outcast of the people.

I have been made a reproach to my neighbours
    exceeding all of my enemies,
and a fear for my acquaintances.

O holy Father, do not keep your help from me,
but look to my defence.

Come to my help,
Lord, God of my salvation.

Psalms 56.1-2; 41.7; 71.10; 41.6; 22.6-7; 31.11; 22.19; 38.22.

A psalm for Terce (mid-morning). Christ, scourged and
crowned with thorns, suffers the mockery and abuse of the
crowd.

I cried to the Lord with my voice;
with my voice I made supplication to the Lord.

I pour out my prayer in his sight,
and I speak of my trouble before him.

When my spirit failed me
you knew my ways.

On the path on which I walked
the proud have hidden a trap for me.

I looked to my right, and I saw,
and there was no one who knew me.

I have no means of escape
and there is no one who cares for my life.

Because of you I have sustained abuse
while confusion covers my face.

I have been made an outcast to my brothers,
and a stranger to the children of my mother.

Holy Father, zeal for your house
    has consumed me,
and the abuses of those
    who have attacked you
    have fallen upon me.

And against me they have rejoiced
    and have united together,
and many scourges were heaped upon me,
    and I knew not why.

More numerous than the hairs of my head
are those who hate me without cause.

Those who persecute me unjustly,
    my enemies, have been strengthened;
must I then restore what I did not steal?

The wicked witnesses who rise up
have interrogated me
    about things of which I am ignorant.

They repaid me evil for good,
    and they harassed me
because I pursued good.

You are my most holy Father,
my King and my God.
Come to my help,
Lord, God of my salvation.

Psalms 142.1-4; 69.7-9; 34.15; 69.4; 35.11-12; 38.20; 44.4; 38.22.

A psalm for Sext, noontide, the hour of the crucifixion.

O all of you who pass along the way,
look and see if there is any sorrow
    like my sorrow.

For many dogs have surrounded me;
a pack of evildoers has closed in on me.

They have looked and stared upon me;
they have divided my garments among them,
    and for my tunic they have cast lots.

They have pierced my hands and my feet;
they have numbered all my bones.

They have opened their mouth against me,
like a lion raging and roaring.

I am poured out like water,
and all of my bones have been scattered.

And my heart has become like melting wax
in the midst of my bosom.

My strength is dried up like baked clay;
and my tongue clings to my jaws.

And they have given gall as my food,
and in my thirst they gave me vinegar to drink.

And they have led me into the dust of death,
and they have added grief to my wound.

I have slept and have risen,
and my most holy Father has received me
    with glory.

Holy Father, you have held
    my right hand,
and you have led me with your counsel.

For what is there in heaven for me,
and besides you what do I want on earth?

See, see that I am God, says the Lord.
I shall be exalted among the nations,
    and I shall be exalted on the earth.

Blessed be the Lord, the God of Israel,
who has redeemed the souls of his servants
    with his very own most holy Blood,
and who will not abandon all who hope in him.

And we know, for he comes,
and he will come to judge justice.

Lamentations 1.12; Psalms 22.13-18; 69.21; 22.15; 69.26; 3.5;
73.24-5; 46.10; Luke 1.68; Psalms 34.23; 96.13.

A psalm for None, the hour of Christ's death.

God, come to my assistance;
Lord, make haste to help me.

Let them be put to shame and confounded
who seek my life.

Let them be put to flight and disgraced
who rejoice at my misfortune.

Let them be turned back in shame
who say to me: Aha! Aha!

May all those who seek you
    exult and be glad in you,
and may those who love your salvation
    ever say:
    'May God be glorified!'

But I am afflicted and poor;
help me, O God.

You are my help and my deliverer;
Lord, do not delay.

Psalm 70.

A psalm for Holy Saturday (at Compline).

Psalms for Easter and the Ascension

Sing to the Lord a new song,
for he has done wondrous deeds.

His right hand and his holy arm
have sacrificed his beloved Son.

The Lord has made his salvation known;
in the sight of the nations
    he has revealed his justice.

On that day the Lord sent his mercy,
and his song at night.

This is the day the Lord has made;
let us rejoice and be glad in it.

Blessed is he who comes
    in the name of the Lord;
the Lord is God,
    and he has given us light.

Let the heavens be glad
    and the earth rejoice,
let the sea and all that is in it
    be moved.
let the fields be joyful
    and all that is in them.

Give to the Lord, you families
    of nations,
give to the Lord glory and praise;
give to the Lord the glory due to his name.

For the Ascension
Sing to the Lord, O kingdoms of the earth;
sing to the Lord.

Chant praise to God who ascends
above the heights of the heavens
    to the east.

Look, he will give his voice
    the voice of power;
give glory to God!
Above Israel is his greatness,
    and his power is in the skies.

God is marvellous in his holy ones;
the God of Israel himself
    will give power and strength to
    his people.
Blessed be God.

Glory to the Father, and to the Son,
    and to the Holy Spirit.

As it was in the beginning,
    is now and shall be forever.
Amen.

Psalms 98.1-2; 42.8; 118.24, 26-7; 96.11-12; 96.7-8; 68.32-5.

A psalm for Matins.

All you nations clap your hands;
shout to God with a voice of gladness.

For the Lord, the Most High, the awesome
is the great King over all the earth.

For the most holy Father of heaven,
    our King before all ages,
has sent his beloved Son from on high
    and has brought salvation
    in the midst of the earth.

Let the heavens be glad
    and let the earth rejoice,
let the sea and all that is in it
    be moved;
let the fields and all that is in them
    be joyful.

Sing a new song to him;
sing to the Lord, all the earth.

For the Lord is great
    and highly to be praised,
and awesome is he beyond all gods.

Give to the Lord, you families of nations,
    give to the Lord glory and honour,
give to the Lord the glory due to his name.

Offer up your bodies and take up his holy cross,
and follow his most holy commands
    even to the end.

Let the whole earth tremble
  before his face;
Say among the nations
  that the Lord has ruled from a tree.

For the Ascension
And he ascended into heaven,
and is seated at the right hand
  of the most holy Father in heaven,
O God, be exalted above the heavens
and above all the earth be your glory.

And we know that he has come,
that he will come to judge justice.

Psalms 47.1-2; 74.12; 96.11-12; 1, 4, 7-8; Luke 14.27; 1 Peter
2.21; Psalms 96.9, 10; 57.11; 96.13.

A psalm for Vespers.

MEDITATE ON
HIS WORD

O how glorious it is,
how holy and great,
to have a Father in heaven.
O how holy, consoling,
beautiful and wondrous,
to have such a Spouse.
O how holy and how loving,
pleasing, humble, peaceful,
sweet, lovable and desirable
    above all things
to have such a Brother
and such a Son;
our Lord Jesus Christ,
who gave up his life for his sheep,
and who prayed to the Father,
    saying:

O Holy Father, protect those in your name
whom you have given to me in the world;
they were yours and you have given them to me.
And the words which you gave to me,
    I have given to them,
and they have accepted them
and have believed truly
    that I have come from you
and they have known that you sent me.
I pray for them
    and not for the world.
Bless and sanctify them,
and I sanctify myself for them.
Not only for these do I pray,
but for those who through their words
    will believe in me,

so that they may be made holy
in being one as we are one.
And I wish, Father,
that where I am
   they also may be with me
so that they may see my glory
   in your kingdom.
Amen.

John 10.5; John 17; Matthew 20.21

From the *Letter to the Faithful*, first version.

Fear and honour, praise and bless, give thanks
    and adore
  the Lord God Almighty in Trinity and in Unity,
  the Father and the Son and the Holy Spirit
  the Creator of all.

Repent, performing worthy fruits of penance
  since we will soon die.

Give and it shall be given to you.

Forgive and you shall be forgiven.

And if you do not forgive men their sins,
  the Lord will not forgive you your sins.
Confess all your sins.

Blessed are those who die in repentance,
  for they shall be in the kingdom of heaven.

Woe to those who do not die in repentance,
  for they shall be the
  children of the devil
  whose works they do,
and they shall go into the eternal fire.

Beware and abstain from every evil
  and persevere in good till the end.

1 Thessalonians 5.18; Matthew 3.2; Luke 3.8; 6.37-8; Matthew
6.14; Mark 11.26; James 5.16; 1 John 3.10; John 8.41; Matthew
18.8.

From the 1221 *Rule of the Friars Minor.*

'Blessed are the peacemakers, for they shall be called the children of God.' The servant of God cannot know how much patience and humility he has within himself as long as everything goes well with him. But when the time comes in which those who should do him justice do quite the opposite to him, he has only as much patience and humility as he has on that occasion and no more.

'Blessed are the poor in spirit, for the kingdom of heaven is theirs.' There are many who, applying themselves insistently to prayers and good deeds, engage in much abstinence and many mortifications of their bodies, but they are scandalised and quickly roused to anger by a single word which seems injurious to their person, or by some other things which might be taken from them. These persons are not poor in spirit because a person who is truly poor in spirit hates himself, and loves those who strike him on the cheek.

'Blessed are the peacemakers, for they shall be called the children of God.' The true peacemakers are those who preserve peace of mind and body for love of our Lord Jesus Christ, despite what they suffer in this world.

'Blessed are the pure of heart, for they shall see God.' The truly pure of heart are those who despise the things of earth and seek the things of heaven, and who never cease to adore and behold the Lord God living and true with a pure heart and soul.

Blessed is that servant who does not pride himself on the good that the Lord says or does through him any more than on what he says or does through another. That person sins who wishes to receive more from his neighbour than what he is willing to give of himself to the Lord God.

Blessed is the person who bears with his neighbour in his weakness to the degree that he would wish to be sustained by him if he were in a similar situation. Blessed is the servant who attributes every good to the Lord God, for he who holds back something for himself hides within himself the money of his Lord God, and that which he thought he had shall be taken away from him.

Blessed is the servant who esteems himself no better when he is praised and exalted by people than when he is considered worthless, simple, and despicable; for what a man is before God, that he is and nothing more.

Woe to that religious who has been placed in a high position by others and does not wish to come down of his own will. And blessed is that servant who does not place himself in a high position of his own will and always desires to be under the feet of others.

Blessed is that religious who takes no pleasure and joy except in the most holy words and deeds of the Lord and with these leads people to the love of God in joy and gladness. Woe to that religious who delights in idle and frivolous words and with these provokes people to laughter.

Blessed is the servant who, when he speaks, does not reveal everything about himself in the hope of receiving a reward, and who is not quick to speak but wisely weighs what he should say and how he should reply. Woe to that religious who does not keep in his heart the good things the Lord reveals to him, and who does not manifest them to others by his actions, but rather seeks to make such good things known by his words. He thereby receives his reward, while those who listen to him carry away but little fruit.

Blessed is the servant who would accept correction, accusation, and blame from another as patiently as he would from himself. Blessed is the servant who when he is rebuked quietly agrees, respectfully submits, humbly admits his fault, and willingly makes amends. Blessed is the servant who is not quick to excuse himself and who humbly accepts shame and blame for a sin, even though he did not commit any fault.

Blessed is the servant who is found to be as humble among his subjects as he would be among his masters. Blessed is the servant who remains always under the rod of correction. He is the faithful and prudent servant, who for all his offences does not delay in punishing himself, inwardly through contrition and outwardly through confession and penance for what he did.

Blessed is the servant who would love his brother as much when he is sick and cannot repay him as he would when he is well and can repay him.

Blessed is the servant who would love and respect his brother as much when he is far from him as he would when he is with him; and who would not say anything behind his back which in charity he could not say to his face.

Where there is charity and wisdom,
    there is neither fear nor ignorance.
Where there is patience and humility,
    there is neither anger nor disturbance.
Where there is poverty with joy,
    there is neither covetousness nor avarice.
Where there is inner peace and meditation,
    there is neither anxiousness nor dissipation.
Where there is fear of the Lord to guard the
      house,
    there the enemy cannot gain entry.
Where there is mercy and discernment,
    there is neither excess nor hardness of heart.

Blessed is that servant who stores up in heaven the good things which the Lord has revealed to him and does not desire to reveal them to others in the hope of profiting thereby, for the Most High himself will manifest his deeds to whomsoever he wishes. Blessed is the servant who keeps the secrets of the Lord in his heart.

The Admonitions, xxii-xxv, xxvii, xxviii.

ACKNOWLEDGEMENTS

Translations of the authentic prayers of St Francis are taken from *Francis and Clare*, translated by Regis J. Armstrong, OFM, CAP, and Ignatius Brady, OFM, from the Classics of Western Spirituality series, copyright © 1982 by The Missionary Society of St Paul the Apostle in the State of New York, USA, and are used by permission of Paulist Press.

Extracts from Thomas of Celano, *The Legend of Perugia* and the *Little Flowers of St Francis* are taken from *St Francis of Assisi, Writings and Early Biographies: English Omnibus of the Sources for the Life of St Francis*, edited by Marion A. Habig, copyright © 1973 by Franciscan Herald Press, Chicago, Ill., USA, and co-published (1979) by SPCK, London:

Thomas of Celano, *The First and Second Life of St Francis*, translated from the Latin by Placid Hermann, OFM

The Legend of Perugia, translated by Paul Oligny from the annotated French version *St Francois d'Assisi: Documents, Ecrits et Premières Biographies* (T. Desbonnets et D. Vorreux, eds., Paris, 1968)

The Little Flowers of St Francis, translated from the Latin and Italian by Raphael Brown (and first published in 1958 by Hanover House, Garden City, NY, USA)